DOGS' LETTERS TO SANTA

COMPILED AND EDITED BY
Bill Adler

ILLUSTRATIONS BY
David Cole Wheeler

Carroll & Graf Publishers
New York

Dogs' Letters to Santa

Carroll & Graf Publishers
An Imprint of Avalon Publishing Group, Inc.
245 West 17th Street, 11th Floor
New York, NY 10011

AVALON

Library of Congress Cataloging-in-Publication Data is available.

ISBN-10: 0-78671-860-9
ISBN-13: 978-0-78671-860-3

9 8 7 6 5 4 3 2 1

Printed in the United States of America
Distributed by Publishers Group West

DOGS' LETTERS
TO SANTA

INTRODUCTION

We all love dogs. And dogs love us.

Now for the first time dogs—small—large—young and old, will have a chance to write to Santa.

Their letters from all over the country are in this book.

Please, Santa—read this book.

Man's best friend wants to have a Merry Christmas.

Bill Adler
New York City
2006

Dear Santa:

Is there a place where dogs can go and pray that you won't forget us this Christmas like you did last year?

Love,
Emma and Bovary
Hastings, NY

Dear Santa Claus:

What did you do before you were Santa Claus?

Did you ever have a real job?

Your fan,
Arthur

Dear Santa:

I love to play with kids.

We only have one kid in our family.

Could you please get me another kid for Christmas?

Love,
Roscoe
Detroit

Dear Santa:

    We love you very much.
    Would you please put us on your very special dogs list?

> Love,
> Claire and Karen
> Washington, DC

P.S. If you can't find a present, we can wait until next year—maybe.

Dear Santa:

    I have written 4 letters to you but so far I haven't heard from you.
    Maybe somebody is stealing your mail.
    I think you need a watchdog.

> Fred
> Seattle

Dear Santa:

Do dogs go to heaven?
I hope so because I don't want to go any place where there are cats.

Your friend,
Rags

Dear Santa:

I would like some goggles please, so when I stick my head out the window of our car to help my person drive, I don't get any more stuff in my eyes.

Desperately,
Edward

P.S. I am very nearsighted.

Dear Santa:

How much does it cost to buy a puppy?
I need a friend in my house.
I have 28 cents. I hope that is okay.

Thank you,
Terry
Memphis

Dear Santa:

You don't have to get me a present for Christmas if you are too busy.

Just send me a picture and your autograph. The autograph should say:

"To my good friend, the smartest dog in Houston."

Everybody will know who you are talking about.

> Sincerely,
> Orson
> Houston

Dear Santa:

I hope you are not too busy to get me a toy for Christmas.

I would like a toy dog or a million dollars. Whichever is easier for you.

> Appreciatively,
> Sandra

Dear Santa Claus:

What time do you get up in the morning?
I have to get up at 5:00 a.m. so the boss in
the house can walk me before he goes to work.
I wish he would get another job.
I need my sleep.

Howie

Dear Santa:

I would like an iPod for Christmas so I could listen to my favorite Backstreet Boys album, without bothering my master.

Yours,
Spike

Dear Santa:

Who is the best dog in the whole world? I hope it is me.

Love,
Pepper
Chicago

P.S. If it isn't me, please don't tell me.

Dear Santa:

I am a boy dog. For Christmas I would like to get a girl dog so next Christmas you can give us some puppies.

Thank you.
Rex

P.S. If you have any ideas please write because I really need my sleep. All I want for Christmas is a good night's sleep.

Dear Santa:

Do you know Donald Trump?
I would like to be on his TV show.
He is very smart and I think he would like me.

Love,
Rocky
Boston

Dear Santa:

My family paid a lot of money for me but I think they got cheated.

The man who sold me at the pet store said I can do a lot of tricks.

Could you send me a book of dog tricks so I won't disappoint them?

Beau

Dear Santa:

They paid $50 for me at the pet store.
I think that was very cheap.
I am worth more than our cat.
They paid $60 for him.

                    Pads
                    Denver

Dear Santa:

If you bite somebody they give my master
a ticket.
I don't think that is fair.
He never bites anyone.

                    Pal
                    Boston

Dear Santa:

I am a Chihuahua and all the big dogs chase me.

Could you send me a big dog for Christmas who will keep the other big dogs away?

Butch
Philadelphia

Dear Santa:

The dog food in my house is great but not if you are hungry. Could you send me some steaks?

Sonny
Buffalo

Dear Santa:

I like to ride on airplanes but they don't let dogs ride on planes so my family hides me in a tennis bag. I would like either a plane ticket, or my own plane.

Someday I will fly to the North Pole to visit you.

Love,
Sylvie
Albuquerque

Dear Santa:

I have seen you in a lot of movies.
You are a better actor than Tom Cruise.

Nikki

Dear Santa Claus:

My daddy needs a new job.
Could you get him a new job as a surprise
Christmas present?
Any job would be okay as long as he
doesn't have to work too hard and he has
enough time to watch TV with me and walk
me and feed me.

Joey

Dear Santa:

What do you do for exercise?
Maybe you should chase squirrels. I
exercise every day when I chase the squirrels
in the neighborhood.

Love,
Ben

Dear Santa Claus:

I am writing for all the dogs in the
neighborhood.
We would like a computer so we can e-mail
messages to each other instead of just barking.

Thank you.
Janet

Dear Santa:

I hope you can help me.
I am allergic to cats and we have 6 cats in our house and I am the only dog.
It doesn't have to be a big dog. Just a puppy who can be my friend.

Love,
Cynthia
San Francisco

Dear Santa:

Please don't leave me any more dog biscuits for Christmas.
I am sick of eating dog biscuits.
How about a Hershey bar?

Love,
Fats

Dear Santa Claus:

There are some dogs in the neighborhood who don't believe in you.
But I believe in Santa so I should get the toys the dogs who don't believe in you would get.

Love,
Zack

Dear Santa:

I never wrote a letter to Santa Claus before.
I hope you like my letter.
Could you send me a letter too?
It doesn't have to be more than 1,000 words.

Asa

P.S. Don't use any big words they didn't
teach in dog obedience school.

Dear Santa:

Could you please find me a home for
Christmas?
The people here at the shelter are very nice
but there are so many of us to take care of that
they don't have time to play or run around.
I would like an owner who has time to
run around.

Coco

Dear Mr. Claus:

The lady of the house always dresses me up when she takes me for a walk.

I am a boy dog and I look silly.

Do you have any sweaters for boy dogs so the other dogs won't laugh when they see me?

Calvin
Age 6

Dear Santa:

There are too many dogs on our block in Brooklyn.

Can't you take some of the dogs from Brooklyn and move them to Las Vegas?

They don't have many dogs in Las Vegas, only short-hairs who don't mind the heat.

Millie

Dear Santa Claus:

Do you know a shrink who could help a very miserable dog who really thinks she is a person?

It isn't me but it is my girlfriend Wanda.

She is very pretty and very smart but she really thinks she is a movie star. Thank you.

Scruffy

Dear Santa:

Who is your favorite dog in the whole world?

I hope it is me.

Love,
Bingo

P.S. I am the favorite dog in this house.
P.P.S. I am also the only dog in this house.

Dear Santa:

Can you send me a doggie bathroom with its own door? I live in New York City and my master and I both find the whole pooper scooper thing completely, horribly humiliating.

Elaine

Dear Santa:

   Do you get a lot of letters from dogs like me?
Maybe you got a letter from Maggie.
   She is the dog in the next house and I think
I love her, but I haven't told Maggie yet
because I also have another girlfriend down
the street.

                        Your friend,
                        Jigs
                        Houston

Dear Santa:

I have been a good dog all year except when I bit the cat by mistake. For the third time.

Your friend,
Frederico
Miami

Dear Santa:

I would like to live with the Sopranos on television. I like that lady with the blonde hair. I don't like the big guy, but she does what he tells her.

Love,
Sparky

Dear Santa:

Please don't leave anything for me under the Christmas tree this year.

Last year the kids took my toy and biscuits.

They are nice kids but they think that kids come before dogs.

Hooper

Dear Santa Claus:

How many dogs do you have in the North Pole?

Do you have room for one more dog?

I'm ready to go except I don't know how to get there.

Could you pick me up?

My address is 280 Park Avenue.

Please come at night so nobody will see me leave.

I am your fan,
Dixie

Dear Santa:

Where do people come up with the crazy names for dogs?

I would rather just be called Mr. Dog than some stupid human name.

Anonymous

Dear Santa:

We have 6 dogs in our family.
I think that is too many dogs.
We are always fighting except when we are sleeping. Can you buy me a ticket to Tahiti?

Your friend,
Bumpy
Brooklyn

Dear Santa:

> Roses are red
> Violets are blue
> If I was a cat
> I don't know what I would do.

> Love,
> Randy, the dog

Dear Santa Claus:

I like people a lot except the people who tell terrible stories about us dogs.

They say that we bite, we bark too much and chase after cars.

It is all a big lie.

I think the lies about dogs were started by the cats.

Walter

Dear Santa:

I read in a dog book that there are 65 million dogs in the U.S.A.

We should elect our own president.

Louie

Dear Santa:

I like to watch TV. I especially like to watch the cooking programs.

The only problem is there aren't any cooking programs on TV for dogs.

Could you find a dog who is a great cook and get her a TV cooking program?

A lot of very hungry dogs will be grateful.

Love,
Julia, the dog

Dear Santa:

I would like to have my own TV/DVD for Christmas so I can watch *Lassie* while everybody else in my house is watching *Everybody Loves Raymond*.

Thank you.

Dear Santa Claus:

We have a new baby in our family.

She is very cute but now everybody in the family hugs and kisses her which is what they used to do to me.

Please take her back.

Caesar
St. Louis

Dear Santa:

Do you like to be called Santa?

Do you have another name?

I wrote a letter to you asking for a new bike for last Christmas but I don't think you got the letter, so I am sending you this letter.

I am desperate for a bike because I hate to walk around the block every morning.

Theodore

Dear Santa:

I have been a perfect dog this year.
I didn't bite anybody and I didn't break anything in the living room.
I hope you remember that when you make up your list of dogs who have been nice and not naughty.

Rodney

Dear Santa:

I need a play date with a poodle.
There aren't any poodles that I know and I love poodles because I am one.

Harvey the Poodle,
Atlanta

Dear Santa Claus:

I hope we have a white Christmas this year so I can ride in the sled.

They pull me on the sled and it is a lot of fun except when I fall off.

Love,
Brownie

Dear Santa:

They built a doghouse for me but I don't like it because it has no TV.

Could you get me a doghouse with a TV?

Thanks,
Smokey

Dear Santa:

I know you know everything.
I have a question:
Which is the smartest dog?
Please write and tell me.

Thank you,
Plato

P.S. I hope it is the golden retriever.

Dear Santa:

Here is a picture of me with my girlfriend. Isn't she cute?

We are going to be married soon and I would like you to come to the wedding.

Everybody else at the wedding will be a dog and you will be the only person.

Yours,
Ranger

Dear Santa Claus:

One of the dogs in the neighborhood told me that people who kiss their dogs are a little nuts.

It's okay to hug a dog but people should kiss people and let the dogs lick each other.

Paddy
Miami

Dear Santa:

Do you have any exercise books for dogs? I would like to get in shape because a bulldog just moved into the neighborhood and I may need protection.

Stanton
Detroit

Dear Santa:

Could you please leave a note that says I don't have to take a bath everyday?
I lick my paws everyday. That's enough.

Love,
Babs

Dear Santa:

Do you know any jobs in this neighborhood where I could make some money and buy a rubber ball that could be mine?
The kids have their own rubber ball but they never let me use it because they say I get it all slobbery.

Hunter

Dear Santa:

If I am sleeping when you come on Christmas Eve, please wake me up.

I don't care how late it is.

I always stay up to watch the late movie.

Nick

Dear Santa:

I have never written a letter to Santa Claus before.

I don't know what to say except I love you, even if you forget to put a toy under the Christmas tree for me like you did last Christmas and the Christmas before and the Christmas before that.

Calvin

Dear Santa:

> I hate to go out in the rain.
> I need a raincoat.
> I think I am a size 2.
>
>> Thank you.
>> Horatio

Dear Santa:

I hope you have lost some weight so you can get down the chimney on Christmas Eve, unlike last year when you had to send us our Christmas gifts by FedEx.

> I'll be waiting.
> Perry, the dog

Dear Santa;

What I really want for Christmas is a new name.

When I was born they called me Butterfly. I think that is a girl's name.

I want them to call me Spike.

A letter from you or even a phone call or an e-mail would be a big help.

When the other dogs ask me my name I tell them I don't know.

> Butterfly
> Detroit

Dear Santa:

I am a dachshund. When it rains, my stomach gets very wet. Could you please make my legs grow?

Love,
Oliver

Hi, Santa:

It's me again.

I'm the dog that wrote you last year for earplugs for Christmas.

I know it was a strange request, but they are always yelling at each other in this house and if I don't get some peace and quiet, I am going to have a breakdown.

If you don't have any earplugs, how about earmuffs?

Katie

Dear Santa:

My best friend is a cat.
Her name is Tiger.
She is a lot of fun.
I think she is in love with me but I don't know how to tell her I'm not a cat.
Could you please let her know so that I won't hurt her feelings?

Thank you.
Wolfie

Dear Santa:

Believe it or not, I would like a canary for Christmas.

They sing pretty and they don't scratch like cats.

I will name the canary after you.

I will call her the Christmas bird.

Freddy

Dear Santa:

The dog in the next house and me always talk to each other over the fence.

The grownups get mad because they think we make too much noise when we talk.

I don't think we make as much noise as they do, but could you send us walkie-talkies?

Bear

Dear Santa:

I have been a good dog all year if you don't think about it.

You don't have to leave me your best present. Just a present for a good dog—me!

Peanut

Dear Santa:

Do they ever put dogs in jail?

If they do, I have the name of a dog that should be in jail.

He lives in the house across the street and he is always chasing cars.

The cars have to get out of his way and one day a car almost hit another car.

He is a very scary dog.

Please take him to another city quick!

Your friend,
Tex

P.S. The dog is my cousin but I still think he should go someplace else.

Dear Santa:

We have 6 dogs in our house.
That is too many.
Should I tell the police?

Andy
Seattle

Dear Santa:

I would like to have dinner in a good French restaurant, even if there are no other dogs there.

Thank you.
Fifi

Dear Santa:

I won't be writing to you anymore.
From now on I will send you an e-mail everyday so you can know what I'm doing.

Raffles

P.S. It may be late at night.

Dear Santa:

I wish I were one of those elephants on television instead of a dog.
Nobody tries to pick on elephants and the kids in this neighborhood are always trying to pick on me. Could you send me a trunk or some tusks?

Rusty
Philadelphia

Dear Santa:

Why can't Emeril write a recipe cookbook for dogs?

Then I could make my own dinner.

Stanley

Dear Santa:

Some dogs are stupid.

They are always chasing after cars and they don't even know how to drive. I don't need to know how to drive, as I have a driver.

Wilma

Dear Santa:

I always sleep in the bed with the family.
Is that okay?
I like it but the only trouble is he snores
and the only way I can stop him is to bark
and then he gets mad.

What should I do?
Lurch

Dear St. Nick:

Which is your favorite kind of dog?
I hope it is a collie because I am one.

Love,
Lassie

Dear Santa:

I think you should have your own TV
show like David Letterman or Oprah.
I would like to be a guest on your show.
I could tell you a lot of funny stories
about dogs I know.

Burryman
the Bassett Hound

Dear Santa:

Here is my picture. You can keep the picture if you send me a box of dog treats or 35 cents.

Love,
Murphy

Dear Santa Claus:

When you were a kid did you always want to be Santa when you grew up?

I am a puppy and I don't know what I want to be when I grow up except maybe a Great Dane instead of a small dog like my sister.

Your fan,
Hilda

P.S. Don't tell my sister about this letter. She doesn't know she is small.

Dear Santa Claus:

Jimmy the cat and me fight all the time.
Sometimes Jimmy wins and sometimes I win.

Could you send me boxing gloves for Christmas so I can win all the time.

Goliath

Dear Santa:

How many Santa Clauses are there in the world?

The reason I am asking is you are everywhere on Christmas Eve.

Did you have a lot of brothers in your litter?

Please write.

Curious

Dear Santa:

They always want me to beg for a dog treat. Have they ever had a dog treat?

If they had, they would certainly know it's not worth interrupting my nap for.

MacGyver
Miami

Dear Santa:

I just found out that my owner had another dog before me. Should I be jealous?

Wadsworth

Dear Santa Claus:

I have been a good dog all year. I even refrained from chasing the new cat in the family.

As my Christmas present, could you please find a new home for the cat?

Hobo

Dear Santa:

I love to play with the kids in the family but they are always pulling at my tail.

Could you send me a toy dog so they can pull at its tail and then they will leave my tail alone?

Thank you.
Roddy

Dear Santa:

I am a sheepdog and I live in the city. I have never seen a sheep. Could you please send me a sheep for Christmas?

Monty

Dear Santa:

I am a herding dog but I have never had anything to herd—do you think you could send me a herd of something for Christmas? They could live in my doghouse with me.

Ozzie

Dear Santa:

I love to play ball with my owner—when he has time, which isn't enough!

Please stop by my house on Christmas Eve and play some ball with me. You don't even have to bring me a present—just a little game of catch would be great.

Murray

Dear Santa:

I like to nap every day at 4:00 p.m. on the sofa in the TV room.

The only trouble is the lady of the house likes to sit on the sofa at 4:00 p.m. every day so she can watch *Oprah*.

I think we need another sofa.

I like *Oprah*, too, but my nap is more important.

Moose

Dear Santa:

I would rather be a cat.
Cats have more fun and they are never on a leash.

Love,
Cody

P.S. Thank you for your help.

Dear Santa:

I don't need any presents from you for Christmas this year. My owner has already bought me a new rubber ball. I sniffed it out in the pile of packages under the tree, but I didn't take it—I know he wants it to be a surprise!

Blue

Dear Santa:

My owners are vegetarians so as you can imagine, the table scraps around here are terrible. Could you please bring me a nice juicy steak for Christmas?

Ty

P.S. Please don't tell my owners about this—they would be so disappointed.

Dear Santa:

I am just a puppy but I would like to be a police dog when I grow up.

For Christmas, would you please bring me a policeman of my own?

Sasha

Dear Santa:

I need a hairnet for Christmas. My lady is saying I shed too much and wants to get a cockapoo and send me to herd sheep. I think it would be very difficult to find time to do this between naps.

Sleepily yours,
Molasses

Hi, Santa:

I wrote to you last year but maybe you didn't get my letter.

So I am sending you another letter.

I hope you get this letter because I am a dog and dogs don't have much money for stamps.

Jayson

Dear Santa:

I am sorry I didn't write to you last Christmas but I was very busy studying so I could graduate from dog obedience school.

I graduated at the head of the class and I was voted the most obedient dog in Scarsdale.

I even got a ribbon.

Brendan

Dear Santa:

Could I get a BlackBerry for Christmas so I could e-mail my best friend Skipper?

If I e-mail him I won't have to bark while they're gone and the neighbors won't complain that I make too much noise.

Rizzo

Dear Santa:

Could you send me a book of dog tricks?
They are always asking me to do a trick
but I need some new ones quick!

Peppy
Albany

Dear Santa:

Do you know Oprah?
All I want for Christmas is to be on the
Oprah program so I can show her some of
my tricks.

You must know Oprah. She would love to
have me on her program.

I do the best dog tricks in the whole city
of Atlanta.

Love,
Jay

Dear Santa:

    I can run very fast.
I am the fastest dog in the neighborhood.
I am even faster than a kid on a bike.

                  Love,
                  Skipper

P.S. I would like roller skates for
Christmas so I can go faster.

Dear Santa:

Will I grow to be a big dog when I get older?

So far, I am 6 and I am very small. Please hurry.

> Love,
> Princess
> Park Avenue

P.S. I'm also always cold, even when it's hot out. Do you think I'm not growing because I'm shivering?

Dear Santa:

If there were more dogs in the world, it would be a better world.

Dogs could protect people so there wouldn't be any crime and dogs could watch over little babies and lick their faces when they cry.

Please remember this letter when you leave your Christmas gifts this year.

Vincent

Dear Santa:

Do you know the names of any vets that give you a treat after they examine you?

The vet I go to pokes me all over and when he is finished he pats me on the head and says, "Good dog."

The truth is I would rather have a treat.

Chili